CW00621375

Tips for Your Barbecue

Tips for Your Barbecue

JIM MARKS

EBURY
PRESS

1 3 5 7 9 10 8 6 4 2

This edition produced for The Book People Ltd.,
Hall Wood Avenue, Haydock, St Helens WA11 9UL

Published in 2008 by Ebury Press, an imprint of Ebury Publishing

A Random House Group Company

The Random House Group Limited Reg. No. 954009

Addresses for companies within the Random House Group can be found at
www.rbooks.co.uk

A CIP catalogue record for this book is available from the British Library

The Random House Group Limited supports The Forest Stewardship Council (FSC),
the leading international forest certification organisation. All our titles that are
printed on Greenpeace approved FSC certified paper carry the
FSC logo. Our paper procurement policy can be found at
www.rbooks.co.uk/environment

Mixed Sources
Product group from well-managed
forests and other controlled sources
www.fsc.org Cert no. TT-COC-2139
© 1996 Forest Stewardship Council

FSC

To buy books by your favourite authors and register for offers visit
www.rbooks.co.uk

Printed and bound in the UK by CPI Mackays, Chatham ME5 8TD

ISBN 978 0 09 1927202

Illustrations by Lizzie Collcutt

CONTENTS

Introduction

The magical combination of fire, food, family, friends and fun explains why barbecuing is such a hit world wide. Its relaxed, outdoor approach to cooking offers a perfect release from the daily drudge. What other social pursuit offers so much pleasure with such great flexibility and so little effort and cost?

You can tackle virtually any type of food on a barbecue and cater for most tastes and occasions – a hearty breakfast or a light lunch, a sophisticated dinner or a cork-popping party, even, in warmer climes, Christmas lunch (freeing up valuable indoor-oven space). You can barbecue almost anywhere too, from the beach to the balcony to the riverbank, on board a boat or in a car park, in the privacy of your patio or garden.

Two personal examples for you to savour. First, a sunny day in the shelter of sand-dunes edging a glorious beach in the Outer Hebrides: I grilled monkfish with scallops, landed that morning, on a small disposable barbecue. Second, a barbecue party in a lakeside apartment in Seattle. Another terrific location and the food – my first taste of buffalo meat – equally sublime. My pal's four-burner gas barbecue, sited on the apartment's balcony, was far removed from the Hebridean disposable, but each was as good as the other. Food cooked on a barbecue not only looks good, smells good and tastes good, but also does you the power of good.

Once bitten by the barbecue bug, not even the weather need stop you: cook out under a covered or lidded barbecue and eat in if it's raining or cold. Any time, any place, anywhere: Happy Barbecuing.

the five golden rules

- Choose a barbecue that suits you (see page 4)

- Invest in the tools that make barbecuing easier (see page 27)

- Find a way to barbecue, whatever the season (see page 37)

- If you can eat it, you can barbecue it (see page 60)

- Remember the merits of the marinade (see page 78)

Buying Your Barbecue

- **Gas, Charcoal or Electric?**
- **Size Matters**
- **Permanent or Portable?**
- **Culinary Ambitions**
- **How Big is Your Budget?**

It makes sense to take a little time to do some basic research before you make up your mind what to buy from the wide range of barbecues available – especially as they often cost as much as a major household appliance such as a dishwasher or refrigerator. Does gas, charcoal- or wood-burning or electric serve your needs best? What size do you need? What are you planning to use it for? It's a lifestyle choice.

Gas, charcoal or electric?

With *gas*, the barbecue is easy to get going – and easy to turn off. It is also ready for use within 5–10 minutes, as well as economical to use. It is easy and precise to control the cooking heat too – and many are self-cleaning. The food tastes, looks and smells just as it does when cooked on a charcoal barbecue.

With *charcoal or wood,* the barbecue experience is seen as somehow more elemental and authentic. Once lit, charcoal will carry on burning steadily. There is the warm, glowing benefit of a real fire. Some people are convinced the food tastes better, but taste tests carried out indicate no significant difference. The choice is strictly personal – although many barbecue zealots beg to differ. Having had a foot in both camps for some time, ever since importing gas barbecues from the States many years ago, I avoid making the choice by constantly swapping and using both types.

Although similar to gas barbecues in that they usually have a volcanic-rock fire-bed, *electric* barbecues are limited simply to grilling meat, fish and vegetables. This, coupled with the fact that they are unavoidably tied to the power source (the nearest dwelling), means they have limited appeal to the barbecue *cognoscenti*. There is also a safety issue in that an overground power cable is a trip-up waiting to happen – especially at night.

Size matters

If you want to use your barbecue for small family cookouts, then a small to medium two-burner portable gas barbecue or perhaps one of the spherical or square-shape charcoal kettle barbecues will probably do nicely. If you are bitten by the barbecue bug and want to use it more frequently, perhaps with a large family plus frequent gatherings of friends, then think how many people you might want to cook for and purchase accordingly. If you want to entertain big numbers of people – and have a pretty deep pocket – why not take a look at one of the large to extra-large wagon gas barbecues – you can get them with as many as eight burners, but, really, the sky's the limit with these impressive-looking units. Increasingly popular are the flat tops, with a large cooking capacity via cast-iron grills and griddle plates mounted into a sturdy hardwood frame. Available as gas or charcoal, although well into the heavyweight class of domestic barbecues they can be moved easily over flat surfaces.

Permanent or portable?

In general, keep your barbecue and your powder (that is your charcoal) dry. It is worth bearing in mind that you may need to have somewhere to store it during the colder months, so you might like to think about choosing something that is portable or can at least be moved and stored easily – and that you have the space in which to store it. Tailored weatherproof covers are usually available for all stay-at-home models. Of course, there is always the built-in option of a permanent outdoor feature.

Culinary ambitions

If your culinary ambition stops short at grilling fast-cooking foods such as burgers, cutlets, chicken portions and fish, then barbecues such as the ubiquitous disposables, braziers and flat tops will fit the bill. If, however, you fancy the idea of roasting and smoke-cooking meats, baking bread, pies and so on, then you will require a barbecue with a lid.

Budget

Set yourself a budget within which to work: a basic gas barbecue or a charcoal brazier won't break the bank, but you can spend, spend, spend on covered wagons, some of which do include the kitchen range! If you are starting from scratch, your budget should include items such as tools and accessories, and, of course, fuel and firelighters.

🔥 Hot Tip
Once you know what you want in terms of fuel preference, cooking capacity, recommended manufacturer and so on, it can pay dividends to shop around for end-of-season deals and special offers.

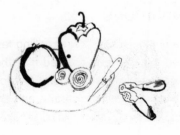

Going with Gas

- **Stay-at-Homes, Portable or Built In?**
- **Fuelling Up**
- **Burner Power**
- **Checklist Before You Buy**

If you are considering a gas barbecue, you are probably going to be looking at a stay-at-home unit, either a flat top or a wagon, though portable versions in all shapes and sizes may suit you better.

Stay-at-homes

Flat tops

These are the versatile and popular all-rounders: models range from two to five burners, each with a cast-metal multi-purpose cooking surface, split between a grill and griddle (usually 50:50 or ⅓:⅔). A pull-out, full-width drip tray, positioned in the base of the barbecue, ensures that the surrounding area, such as your patio, stays grease free. A flat, full-size lid is provided against bad weather, pets and pests.

> 🌢 **Hot Tip**
>
> *Some flat tops can be converted to a wagon (covered barbecue) by fitting a roasting hood.*

Wagons (covered barbecues)

These come in a wide range of sizes, power and capacities. The smallest have a cooking area of about 200 sq cm (32 sq inches) and the largest up to 4,000 sq cm (640 sq inches). All bar the smaller models usually

have a heat indicator mounted in the lid and include a warming rack.
Power ratings vary from 11,000 BTU (3 kW) to 50,000 BTU (14.5 kW).

Portable gas barbecues

These are great for holiday use with the added bonus that they can be
pressed into service at the drop of a hat as a valuable back-up for
general cooking duties at large cookouts. Models vary in weight, power,
design and cooking proficiency. The lightweight units are, in general,
powered by universally available disposable gas cartridges. The smallest
cartridges provide approximately one and a half hours' cooking time.
Most portable units can be hooked up to standard gas cylinders, which
not only makes the barbecue more economical to run but also, more
importantly perhaps, less likely to run out of gas mid-cookout.

> ### 🔥 Hot Tip
> *Remember to pack spare gas cartridges when heading for
> that lonely picnic spot miles from anywhere.*

Built-in gas barbecues

Gas barbecues suitable for this kind of use range from wagons (minus their undercarriage) to flat tops (minus their trolley). The setting structure, usually brick or stone, is permanent, but the barbecue itself is removable for storage.

Fuel

Gas barbecues can be used with butane, propane or natural gas. The operating pressures for the different types of bottled gas are different, so you should use the correct regulator. It is not possible to change from one gas to the other without changing the regulator. Natural gas would be the ideal fuel for permanent built-in barbecues, but installing an underground supply pipe must be carried out by a fully qualified Corgi-approved or equivalent tradesman.

> ### ✎ Hot Tip
> *As a rule the greater a barbecue's BTU/kW rating the better. Dividing the rating by the area of the cooking surface will provide an indication of the barbecue's cooking power. Around 15.5 BTUs per square cm/100 BTUs per square inch is good.*

Burners

The burner is to the gas barbecue as the engine is to your car, and, as with cars, there is a big variation in quality, performance and durability. In addition to the *main burner*, some wagons have an extra outside or *side burner* mounted next to the hood: these are very useful, allowing you to prepare soups, veg, sauces and hot drinks while cooking the main event. The more powerful the better, the side burner is ideal for locating a small wok and doing some stir-frying, braising, deep-frying or steaming.

Another added extra, the *rotisserie burner*, is supplied with the more expensive wagon units. Located at the rear of the grill area, the heat radiating from it reaches the rotating meat from behind, allowing the fats and juices to fall into a drip pan. Another benefit is that you can spit-roast with the hood of the barbecue shut, which is extremely efficient, particularly in windy weather.

 WARNING
Never attempt to move a gas barbecue when its burners are alight.

going with gas

Checklist before you buy

✔ Look out for a sticker indicating CE-Approved (for the European market) or recommended by the official approval authority in North America and other countries. If in doubt, confirm safety and technical credentials with the retailer.

✔ Note whether the burner controls are conveniently situated.

✔ Test whether the barbecue is stable. See if it is easy to manoeuvre.

✔ Ensure there is sufficient volcanic rock or ceramic briquettes provided – enough to cover the fire-grate in a single, crowded layer. A smallish gap around the grate perimeter is fine; anything large could let fat drop directly on to the burners and cause a flare-up.

✔ Make sure the barbecue has a sturdy and good-size work surface, big enough to take a chopping board, condiments and other essentials.

Choosing Charcoal or Wood

- **Portable or Stay-at-Home?**
- **Checklist Before You Buy**
- **Fuel and Firelighters**

If you are considering a traditional charcoal- or wood-fuelled barbecue, you are spoilt for choice. There are many different models available, which can be roughly divided into portable and improvised and stay-at-home, 'I'm too heavy and awkward for you to get me into the car boot' models.

Portable and improvised

These are perfect for use away from home by picnickers, backpackers, campers, caravanners and the like. They include disposable barbecues, picnic barbecues, hibachis and beach barbecues.

Disposable barbecues

The practical choice for anyone travelling light. Disposables are compact, lightweight and economically priced. Generally available in three sizes, they comprise a shallow foil tray containing lumpwood charcoal (about 20–30 minutes' cooking time), a sheet of lighting paper and a grill made from expanded metal. These very handy little barbecues can be refuelled and placed in a carrier bag (to prevent the charcoal dust from spreading) for further use.

Picnic barbecues

There are many models and ingenious designs from which to take your pick. Most are simply scaled-down versions of bigger barbecues, with similar features, such as windshields and adjustable grills. Some have lids for sheltering food during grilling and creating a compact unit that is easy to transport. Most lids, however, are too shallow to allow indirect-heat cooking (that is, they are no good for roasting or baking). Those with fold-down or clip-on legs are more comfortable for cooking than 'legless' versions that sit on the ground.

Hibachis

From the Japanese word for fire-box, fire-bowl or brazier, the sizes of these cast-metal or pressed-steel barbecues varies from a mere 10–12 cm (4–5 inches) to a circular version around 41 cm (16 inches) in diameter.

Beach barbecues

Along with biscuit tins, ploughshares (claimed by South Africans as the best on which to prepare their own traditional barbecue cookout, a *braai*) and oil drums, why not make your own? Start by scooping out a well/fire-bowl a few inches deep in the sand. Open up a channel to the well from the side hit by the prevailing wind to let air reach the base of the fire. Set a spaced ring of large, dry stones around the edge of the well/fire-bowl to act as a windbreak and grill support. Use driftwood as fuel, allowing it to burn down to hot embers before cooking. Try chicken wire as a temporary grill, doubled over to reduce the size of the holes and increase rigidity (burn off its galvanised coating before grilling your food on it). Alternatively, use a stainless-steel cake cooling rack. Select your barbecue site carefully, especially if the beach is fairly crowded. Take care to do this well away from anything that might catch fire, and when you're done, be sure to put out the fire properly. By late evening you will probably have the beach pretty much to yourself.

Stay-at-homes

These are ideal for use at home or, in any case, in a permanent, fixed position.

Chiminerias

Apart from posing as an interesting piece of garden sculpture, the chimineria burns both charcoal and wood. After cooking, with the addition of a bit more wood, it can double as a patio heater. Available in cast aluminium, cast iron and handmade cast clay (check for frost-proofing), the fire-grate and cooking grill are usually made from cast iron. These ultra-heavy cooking units should be sited on a level base or firm, level ground, but not directly on to wooden decking without adequate protection against scorching.

Braziers

These are open-top units, rectangular or circular, with or without wheels, generally made from sheet or cast metal. Braziers invariably incorporate a windshield specifically designed to support a rotisserie. Some have a grill that rotates freely on an axis; with most models the grill has to be adjusted via variable height slots on the windshield. Braziers are generally easy to dismantle and transport.

Flat tops

Flat tops comprise a significant and fast-growing proportion of the open tops. With their cast-iron grills and griddle plates set in a sturdy hardwood trolley, these heavyweight units look strikingly similar to gas-burning models. They feature full-width, easily removable ash pans and adjustable charcoal baskets (for heat control); despite large wheels and casters for ease of manoeuvre, they spend the whole of their working life at their home base.

choosing charcoal or wood

Covered barbecues

If you want to do more than basic cooking – to roast and bake a wide and interesting variety of food and even smoke-cook meat and fish – you will need to consider buying a barbecue with a vented lid. The kettle is one of the most popular covered barbecues available: a spherical kettle has a grill and grate in a permanently fixed position; a square kettle features a grill that is adjustable to various heights and, usefully, inclinations, as well as sometimes incorporating a rotisserie.

Smokers

This is a multipurpose barbecue that resembles an oversize cigar tube. The majority have two cooking grills sited one above the other, in the top half of the cylindrical body. The size of the cylindrical body is generally about 45 cm (18 inches) in diameter and 100 cm (40 inches) high, enough space to handle meat up to 22 kg (50 lb) in weight. So, you could smoke a ham on one of the grills and a turkey on the other.

Situated in the base is a pan to hold charcoal, directly above which is the water pan. A small door at the side allows easy refuelling. The smoker can be used for traditional grilling and roasting, but comes into its own when cooking meat in the moist steam generated by waves of moderate heat striking the water pan.

choosing charcoal or wood

Wagons

These are the largest of the covered barbecues; the bigger ones can cope with the flat-food (burgers, steaks and so on) demands of large parties and/or joints of meat. Certain ultra-heavyweight wood-burning models – recognised by their smokestacks and large wagon wheels – are capable of handling and smoke-cooking huge quantities of food. Known as pit barbecues in the USA, they are now available, and becoming increasingly popular, throughout western Europe due to their ability to smoke-cook meat to perfection. Most have a heat indicator in the lid, useful for more precise baking and roasting. Some have a retractable warming rack that swings back with the lid when it is opened, which is more user friendly than a rack set in a fixed position.

Built-in charcoal barbecues

These are readily available in DIY kit form: a chrome-plated grill, fire-grate, ash/fat tray and support brackets. They come with detailed instructions on how to build a rectangular supporting brick structure, usually requiring around 100 bricks.

Checklist before you buy

✔ Stability: give the unit a nudge to see if it wobbles unduly – don't forget that it will need to support a fully laden grill, plus a charcoal fire-bed.

> ### 🔥 Hot Tip
> *A wobbly barbecue could be due to poor assembly, so bear that in mind when testing before you buy and then again when you assemble your new barbecue unit at home.*

✔ With any chrome-plated grill, ensure there are no thin or bare patches.

✔ With any adjustable-height grill supported by the windshield (the deeper the windshield the better), check that the grill slots easily into the shield, bearing in mind that it will, at some stage, be fully laden and heavy to handle.

✔ With any covered barbecue, make sure the lid fits snugly and is not distorted. Ensure that the lid's air vent(s) is easy to adjust.

✔ With any mechanism for raising/lowering the grill, check how smoothly it operates.

✔ Spacing: ensure the grill bars are spaced closely enough to prevent food, such as small sausages and chicken wings, falling through.

✔ Sharp edges: make sure there are none – to the lid, fire-box or ash-pan.

Which fuel?

The choice is between charcoal and wood.

Charcoal

Quality is key. Why not try different brands until you find one that fits the bill – success hinges on charcoal that is relatively easy to get started, capable of providing a good heat level and takes a long time to burn. You can buy it as lumpwood or briquettes.

Lumpwood charcoal should be bone dry and feel light for its bulk with minimal residual dust left in the bag. The best is made from hardwoods, such as beech, but it is not uncommon for some softwood to be included. Its main advantage is that it is relatively easy to light.

Charcoal briquettes are made from pulverised material, to which a starch is added to bind into shape. Their main advantage is that they burn for twice as long as lumpwood charcoal, making them suitable for long cooking. Their main disadvantage is that they can be difficult to ignite, though *instant-lighting charcoal* can be ready for use some 20 minutes after the paper bag in which it is packed is lit.

Hot Tip
Never add instant-lighting charcoal briquettes to an established fire. The fumes they give off initially from the ignition agent will adulterate any food on the grill.

Sustainable charcoal, burnt in kilns from managed woodlands where trees grow back in a few years, is worth considering.

Wood

You can use virtually any well-seasoned hardwood: beech is most readily available, followed by oak, birch, ash, apple and cherry. Vine cuttings are easy to light, but you will require a lot of them to produce sufficient cooking heat, so they're most suited to fast-cooking foods such as small fish, cutlets or chicken wings.

Which firelighters?

There are several options from which you can choose, among them:

Solid firelighters Widely used for many years to keep the home fires burning and now popular for barbecues. The black smoke and the odour dissipate before the fire is ready to cook on. A smokeless version of the block firelighter is available: non-toxic, odourless and clean burning.

Liquid firelighters Specifically for the barbecue: non-volatile, but not for adding to a lit fire.

WARNING

Never use petrol, methylated spirits, lighter fluid, kerosene, naptha or similar volatile liquids to light your fire. never add more starter fluid to a lighted charcoal or wood fire, even if it appears not to be burning. use a solid firelighter to rekindle. if in any doubt, the safe option is to start the fire again from scratch.

Jellied alcohol (lighter paste) Very convenient starter for picnic barbecues – but more expensive than the rest.

Compact blow torch Gives a good result but requires you to be on hand for a few minutes until the fire takes hold.

Charcoal chimney This is a metal tube with a handle attached, roughly 15 cm (6 inches) in diameter and 30 cm (12 inches) long, that you place in the barbecue grate. Stuff the bottom with crumpled newspaper, top up with charcoal then set light to the paper. Allow about 15 minutes for the charcoal to ignite, then carefully remove the chimney and spread out the charcoal as required.

Gadgets and Gizmos

- **BBQ Basic Kit**
- **BBQ Extras: A–Z**

If you're new to the game, concentrate on what makes barbecuing easier and safer, such as tongs, gloves and forks. When you get more of a bee in your bonnet about the BBQ lifestyle, you can build up your bank of equipment to keep the fun in barbecuing yet make sure it's as foolproof as possible.

BBQ basic kit

You shouldn't even think about starting to barbecue without these three basic items.

Forks
Anything long-handled with a comfortable wooden or PVC grip is your best buy.

Gloves
Go for gloves rather than mitts – and gauntlets rather than gloves (to protect the lower forearm). Try them on to make sure you can grip tools firmly and comfortably; heat-resistant padding is vital.

Tongs

A good pair of tongs is the most important tool in the barbecue cook's arsenal. You'll need a pair that not only suits your hand's strength and size but also enables you to be dextrous with chipolatas.

BBQ extras: A–Z

Consider treating yourself to some of these barbecue add-ons – with experience, you'll discover how useful they can be.

Apron

For comfort and practicality, nothing beats a cotton apron, ideally knee-length with a couple of pockets for kitchen roll, etc. Any plastic-coated apron is like wearing a raincoat in a sauna.

Basting brushes

Long-handled basting brushes are available, but some cooks prefer a couple of good-quality 5 cm (2 inch) paint brushes, one to apply the oils, the other to apply the sauces. Bristles should be natural, not nylon or man-made.

Bug repellent

For warm summer evenings, an insect-repellent spray, citronella candle or electronic zapper is a worthwhile investment.

Burn lotion

A small burn or blister is par for the course in any busy barbecue year, so a spray-on burn lotion is a useful addition to your first-aid kit.

Chopping boards

The larger the better, generally, and, ideally, either plastic or laminate.If you opt for good-quality hardwood, make sure you scrub it well after each use.

Cleaning brushes for the grill and griddle pan

The best and cheapest grill cleaner is a simple kitchen-foil ball. You can get grill-cleaning brushes, but their fine-wire bristles invariably clog up with fat and food debris, leaving you to clean the cleaning brush. Where they are useful is for the metal scraper blade that most of them have, handy for scraping off burnt-on fatty deposits on the upper and lower housings and the griddle pan.

Drip pans

For roasting meat: either buy one, a standard steel roasting tin or a light-weight aluminium drip pan, or make one yourself, double-thickness, from a roll of foil (which can be binned afterwards, once the fat has congealed).

Make your own drip pan

Take an 46 cm (18 inch) roll of extra-thick aluminium foil and tear off a strip about 7.5 cm (3 inches) longer than the length of the pan you need. Fold the foil in half lengthwise, shiny side out.Use a piece of wood, or the side of a book, to help form the side and end walls of the pan which should be about 2.5–4 cm (1–1.5 inches) in from the edge. Pull out the corners as shown in the sketch, and fold back tightly against the sides. The result should be a leak-proof tray approximately 15 cm (6 inches) wide with sides 2.5–4 cm (1–1.5 inches) high.

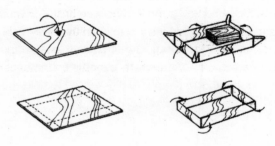

Gas lighters/gas matches

If you have a gas barbecue that does not incorporate a Piezo or push-button igniter, these are handy to own – and perfect in any case as back-up. Also useful for lighting solid firelighters, garden flares and so on.

Holders: fish

These are holders designed for handling fish, which can be particularly fragile when partially cooked and in need of turning. For single fish: the most common accommodate a fish weighing up to 375 g (12 oz), such as a trout, and the largest a fish of 1 kg (2 lb). Another version holds three fish, each around 375 g (12 oz), side by side. A holder that looks like a bicycle wheel takes up to 12 little fish, such as sardine.

Holders: hinged wire

Chrome-plated, these square, rectangular or round wire holders, well oiled, are good for handling small chicken wings or livers or cocktail sausages, enabling you to turn over several of them in one go. The ones with pockets are good for burgers or chops or for toasting bread or buns; the cylindrical or rectangular box-shape ones are good for clamping to a spit rod, so small pieces of food can tumble and spit-roast freely.

Kitchen foil

Aluminium kitchen foil is indispensable, for making a temporary drip pan or griddle plate and for cleaning. Try to keep a supply of the heavy-duty variety.

Kitchen paper

Vital for mopping spills and brows, spreading oil over fish and grill bars, wrapping around hot sausages or wiping sticky fingers.

Knives and cutlery

A good-quality butcher's knife for meat, small paring knife for fruit and veg, sharp carving knife for roasts. Avoid plastic cutlery with most meats.

Meat thermometer

Great for taking the guesswork out of cooking larger joints and particularly useful for assessing whether a joint of pork is fully cooked. A false reading will occur if the tip of the pointed probe touches bone or spit rod. Avoid leaving the thermometer in the meat during the cooking process as the glass may shatter.

gadgets and gizmos

Paint scraper

The professional's choice for removing food debris and fat from griddle plates. Treat yourself to one for culinary use only.

Pots and pans

Thick bases with long handles are best, which, if wooden or plastic, can be wrapped in foil to protect them. For domestic harmony, consider buying one or two solely for barbecue use.

Rotisseries or spit-roast assembly

If not standard, most manufacturers include one in their range.

Skewers

Metal skewers with a flat or twisted blade are best for spearing meat or veg. Twin-pronged ones are best for holding food firmly in position.

> ### ✐ Hot Tip
> *Soak bamboo or wooden skewers in water before use to prevent them catching light or burning up before the food is fully cooked.*

Spatulas

Long-handled with broad, slotted blade for free draining of fat is preferable; the scissor action of the twin-bladed spatula is best for gripping and positioning food.

Woks

Look out for a wok that includes a set of tools – a ladle and shovel – and check that the wok is the right size for your barbecue before you buy. A gas side burner is considered best for wok-cooking.

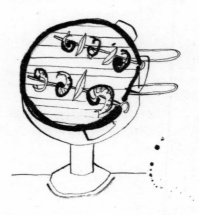

Light Your Fire

- **Safety First: Read the Manufacturer's Instructions**
- **Dos and Don'ts: Gas**
- **Dos and Don'ts: Charcoal/Wood**
- **Heat Control and Flare-ups**

Manufacturer's instructions

Safety first! You are home with your new barbecue and raring to go. But, before you use it, your first task is to read the operating manual, on safety and how to bring out the best in your new purchase.

Getting started: gas barbecues

You might like to start with some basic dos and don'ts.

First the dos

Carry out a leak test before fitting the hose, valve and regulator. All of these are normally supplied interconnected, although with some models you may need to supply and fit the regulator to the barbecue's control panel.

> **LEAK TEST**
> *MAKE up a soap and water solution. TAKE your full gas cylinder and the hose, valve and regulator assembly outside and connect the regulator to the cylinder valve. TURN the control knob(s) of the barbecue valve(s) to Off. TURN on the gas supply at the cylinder. APPLY the soapy water to all*

*the connection points, from, and including, the cylinder
valve to the valve(s) at the end of the hose. CHECK each
connection point for bubbles caused by leaks. Tighten any
leaky connections (replacing any item that leaks
persistently). TURN off the gas supply at the cylinder and
turn the control knob(s) to High to release the pressure in
the hose. Disconnect the regulator from the cylinder and fit
the assembly to the barbecue according to the
manufacturer's instruction.*

Make sure you have a match or a taper ready to light the gas before turning it on.

Fully close the cylinder valve when the barbecue is not in use.

Store the cylinder outdoors in a well-ventilated place.

Keep the cylinder upright at all times.

Open the lid of the barbecue before lighting the gas burners.

Allow a space of at least 75 cm (30 inches) between the barbecue and any flammable material, such as wood, etc.

Keep children and pets well away from all hot barbecues.

Now the don'ts

Store the gas cylinder in direct sunlight.

Smoke or use a naked flame when testing for gas leaks.

Store or use petrol, or any other volatile liquids or vapours, near the barbecue.

Adjust your gas barbecue indoors or in any confined, unventilated area.

Move a gas barbecue when it is lit.

Troubleshooting guide: gas burners

At some point, you will hit a snag. What follows are some common problems – and solutions – to help keep you on track. The manufacturer's operating booklet for your model should indicate where the venturi tube and other components are located.

Burners will not light
Possible cause: The cylinder of gas is almost empty.
Solution: Replace with a full cylinder.

Possible cause: The cylinder valve is not fully open.
Solution: Fully open the cylinder valve (turn the valve anti-clockwise).

Possible cause: The valve outlets are not properly seated in the venturi.
Solution: Fully locate the valve in the venturi (when properly in position, the gas jets are visible through the venturi 'window').

Possible cause: One or more of the gas jets or venturis is clogged (perhaps with spider webs or cocoons).
Solution: Clean the inside of the venturi tubes with a bottle brush. Carefully clean the jet orifices with fine wire or the tip of a round tooth pick – do not enlarge the hole.

Possible cause: The venturis are not properly seated.
Solution: Check that the retaining spring, if used, is properly engaged.

Possible cause: A sharp kink in the flexible gas hose.
Solution: Re-position the cylinder to straighten the hose.

light your fire

Possible cause: The igniter is not working.
Solution:
1. Check assembly instruction to ascertain if the gap between the electrode cover is correct (if it is, a spark should be visible).
2. Ensure all wires are intact and connected.
3. Check the ceramic component for cracks (if a new igniter assembly is required, use a long taper in the meantime).

Possible cause: A defective value or regulator.
Solution: If you suspect either of the above is faulty, remove the hose from the barbecue and take it, along with the regulator and cylinder, to an authorised servicing bottle-gas dealer for inspection.

Burners provide insufficient heat
Possible cause: The barbecue is not given sufficient time to warm up.
Solution: Increase the warm-up time by several minutes to allow for low air temperatures and strong breezes.

Possible cause: The venturis and gas jets are not properly aligned.
Solution: Fully locate the valve in the venturi.

Possible cause: Some of the vents in the burner assembly are clogged with food debris.
Solution: Brush clean (using a brass or stainless-steel bristle brush).

Possible cause: An excessive amount of volcanic rock is used.
Solution: Remove sufficient rock to allow a close-packed single layer only.

Possible cause: One or more of the gas jets or venturis is clogged.
Solution: Clean the inside of the venturi with a bottle brush. Carefully clean the jet orifices with fine wire or the tip of a fine toothpick (taking care not to increase the hole size).

Possible cause: The volcanic rock is permeated with food debris and fat.
Solution:
1. Wash the rocks in hot water, to which a biological soap (powder or tablet) solution has been added. Change the water and repeat as necessary. Make sure the volcanic rock is thoroughly dry before using it for cooking. Dry it either in the barbecue with the lid down or in the kitchen oven.
2. Or, burn the rocks clean (see Cleaning your Barbecue, page 73).

Flashback (flame in or around the venturi)

If flashback occurs, immediately shut off the barbecue burner controls and then turn off the cylinder valve.

Possible cause: The venturis have become hot when the barbecue has cooled.
Solution: Clean the inside of the tube with a bottle brush.

Possible cause: The venturis are not properly seated.
Solution: Check that the retaining spring (if used) is present and engaged.

Possible cause: The valve outlets are not properly seated in the venturi.
Solution: Fully locate the valve in the venturi.

Possible cause: The vents in the burner assembly are clogged.
Solution: Brush clean, using a brass or stainless-steel bristle brush (or a piece of fine wire or a round toothpick).

Possible cause: The barbecue is exposed to strong winds.
Solution: Shield the middle/lower half of the barbecue from the wind (or turn off the gas and move the barbecue to a more sheltered position).

Burner flame is excessively yellow

Possible cause: The burner holes are clogged.
Solution: Brush clean with a brass or stainless-steel bristle brush.

Possible cause: The venturi tubes are blocked.
Solution: Clean the inside of the venturi tubes with a bottle brush.

Possible cause: The venturis are not properly located on the valve outlets.
Solution: Check that the retaining spring, if used, is properly engaged.

Barbecue hot spots

The shape, size and location of your gas barbecue's burners (in relation to the cooking area they are serving), plus their power output, greatly influence the manner and speed in which your food will cook. Experience will eventually make you aware of where the hot, medium and cool spots are located on the grill. But Jim's Toast Test is an easy and tasty way to ascertain the heat distribution pattern of your new gas barbecue: its fingerprints.

Jim's Toast Test

All you need is a loaf of sliced white bread and a calm day or a sheltered spot. If you do the test around tea time, why not take out butter and jam too, so the whole family can enjoy their toast al fresco – your first barbecue experience.

Light the burners. Close any lid. Leave the barbecue to warm up for about 10 minutes. Adjust the control knob(s) to medium and leave for 2–3 minutes more. Open the lid (if relevant) and cover the entire surface of the grill(s) with the bread then leave for 2 minutes or until the underside is nicely browned. Using tongs, turn each slice where it sits and see, by the colour gradation, where the grill is hottest and where it's coolest.

Mission accomplished, spread your toast with lashings of butter and jam. Enjoy!

Heat control: gas

Once the barbecue is up to temperature, you can concentrate on the food. But try to keep an eye on the heat. With a gas barbecue, of course, it is controllable in an instant.

Getting started: the charcoal fire-bed

What's the best way to get the fire going? That depends on whether you're grilling or spit-roasting, baking or smoke-cooking.

Grilling, wok or griddle-plate cooking

Build a pyramid-shape pile of charcoal in the centre of the fire-grate.

If using *solid firelighters*, insert two or three pieces into the lower half of the pile. After lighting, the starter will burn for about 15 minutes, depending on the type of barbecue and the wind strength. When most of the coals are covered by a grey ash, spread them over the grate one layer deep (if wok-cooking, leave the pyramid intact), and leave until all are blanketed in ash. You can now start to cook.

> ### ✍ Hot Tip
> *During the early stages of firelighting, particularly if the wind is up, keep an eye on the firelighters to see they are burning well and have not gone out.*

If using *liquid firelighters*, carefully follow the manufacturer's instructions. Take care not to use too much liquid, particularly with barbecues that incorporate air vents in their fire-bowl, as excess liquid may drain out of the barbecue and accidentally ignite.

If using *jellied firelighters*, squeeze small amounts into cavities near the base of the charcoal pyramid. Close and remove the tube, and light the jelly as soon as possible.

If using a *gas torch*, arrange the charcoal on the grate one layer deep and closely together. Light the gas and adjust the flame, then play the flame slowly over the fuel until grey patches appear.

Spit-roasting
Position a pile of charcoal on the fire-grate towards the rear of the fire-bowl and light as described above.

Roasting, smoke-cooking and baking by 'indirect heat' (covered barbecues only)
Ensure the lower vents are fully open. Place a pan, such as an old roasting tin, in the centre of the fire-grate; if using a round 'kettle' model, clip the charcoal retention rails into position. Place two solid firelighters about 10 cm (4 inches) apart on each side of the grate, cover them with briquettes (around 40 per side for a Sunday roast) and light with a long

match or taper. Depending on the number of firelighters used and wind strength, the fire should become established in 30–60 minutes.

> **Hot Tip**
> *If you are in a hurry to light your fire, double up the firelighters.*

Heat control: charcoal/wood

With the fire burning steadily, you are now free to concentrate on cooking and controlling the heat to suit. With a charcoal- or wood-burning barbecue, it's a less-than-exact science, but these handy hints should help.

ADJUST the lower air vents in a covered barbecue (the vent in the lid of a covered barbecue should always be left open during cooking).

ALTER the distance between the fire-bed and grill by means of rotating grills, adjustable levers and so on.

INCREASE or decrease the distance between the charcoal once it is alight: the closer the lumps of fuel, the hotter the fire.

light your fire

TAP OFF excess ash (rapping the rim of the barbecue's fire-bowl should do the trick) to produce a small surge in temperature; leave the ash in place to dampen an overly hot fire.

🌶 Hot Tip

Keep a reserve of briquettes near but not quite touching the live coals. Cold briquettes, when added directly to hot coals will, momentarily, dampen down the fire.

Flaming flare-ups

Avoid flare-ups like the plague – they are not inevitable. One of the problems is that, unless you react fast, they can spoil the appearance of the food, covering it with a greasy, black film.

The worst flare-ups are created by excessive heat striking excessively fatty food. Unless you react quickly the fat falling on the fire-bed will boost the flames into a mini-inferno. You should know that gas barbecues can also develop flare-ups, which are a little easier to manage, because you are more in charge of the barbecue controls.

How to avoid charcoal/wood flare-ups

Cover one-third of the grate with charcoal crowded closely together. Cover another third with fuel set about 5 cm (2 inches) apart. Leave one-third of the grill vacant. In the event of a flare-up you can move the food to the vacant lot, using a pair of tongs. This is also useful if you want to cook meat rare, medium or well done. You can set aside an order for a rare steak on the vacant lot while continuing to cook the rest of the food.

Another fat/flare-up reducing exercise: part-cook chicken pieces or large sausages in a roasting tin in the oven or a covered barbecue for about 30 minutes so that they lose much of their fat. Keep the partly cooked food covered and cool until you are ready to grill it on the barbecue.

🔥 Hot Tip
Tilt the barbecue slightly towards the vacant lot, with grill bars facing the same direction. This way, some of the fat/juices will trickle down the bars into a pre-positioned drip pan.

Snuffing out the fire

Try not to waste charcoal – snuff it out when you're through. With covered barbecues, the fire will be cold in about 30 minutes if you close the top and bottom dampers. With open barbecues, you can either transfer the charcoal carefully to a lidded metal coal bucket or dump it in a pail of water for later draining and drying.

 WARNING

Tempting as it may be, never pour water over hot charcoal in the barbecue as this might damage the unit.

Safety First!

- **Tips for Fire Safety**
- **Tips for Food Safety**

To make your barbecue memorable for the right reasons: play it safe when playing with fire and food.

Tips for fire safety

Never leave a hot barbecue unattended.

Keep lit barbecues away from combustibles such as trees and dry shrubbery, wooden sheds, fences.

Keep small children, always fascinated by fire, well away from a lit barbecue – as well as any meandering 'happy' adults.

Know where your fire extinguisher is – and keep a bucket of water or sand or a garden hose close by just in case shrubbery or fencing catch alight.

> ✍ **Hot Tip**
> *Never use water to douse a flare-up as this could warp and damage the barbecue.*

With closed units, in case of a flare-up, close off the vents and replace the lid.

Always use good-quality heat-resistant gloves or gauntlets and long-handled tools when tending the fire and turning the food.

Mount the barbecue on a flat surface (preferably non-slip) leaving adequate space around it for people to circulate freely – important if the food is being passed out directly to guests from the barbecue through-out the evening.

Site the drinks/cutlery and condiments tables well clear of the barbecue.

Burning charcoal emits carbon monoxide, so never light or use your barbecue in a confined space such as a garage.

Make doubly sure that any hot coals remaining from your picnic barbecue are fully extinguished before leaving the site. Needless to say, tidy up and leave the area as you found it. At home, when you have finished cooking on your covered charcoal-burning barbecue, put on the lid and shut all vents.

safety first!

Tips for food safety

Food poisoning bacteria can be found almost everywhere. If you follow these simple guidelines, you should minimise any risk of food poisoning.

Before preparing the food and starting to barbecue, wash your hands thoroughly, using soapy water as hot as you can handle. Hand-washing is particularly important after handling fresh meat, poultry or fish.

✎ Hot Tip
Clean hands, safe food.

Thaw frozen meat and fish in a cool room or in a refrigerator, allowing sufficient time for the poultry to defrost fully before cooking. A bird will be ready for cooking when its body is pliable, its legs move freely in its joints and the body cavity is free from ice crystals. Once fully thawed, keep poultry in the refrigerator and cook within 24 hours.

When defrosting, ensure that none of the juices escapes on to work surfaces or drips on to other food.

Any work surfaces touched by the meat or fish juices should be wiped with an antibacterial cleaning liquid.

Keep raw and cooked entirely separate: never place cooked food on the same plate/dish as raw food at any time.

Similarly, when handling raw and cooked food, use separate cooking utensils, preferably even aprons, as well as work surfaces. In an ideal barbecue world, you would have two sets of everything – in varying shapes, colours and sizes for easy identification.

Make sure all food is cooked through, especially poultry, burgers and sausages. If you pierce poultry meat with a fork or skewer, the emerging juices should run clear, not pink. Burgers or similar products should be cooked through until their centres are piping hot with no hint of pink.

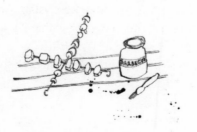

How to Cook

- **Grills and Kebabs**
- **Roasts, Bakes, Spit-roasts and Smoke-cooking**
- **Wok-cooking/Stir-fries**
- **Cooking in Foil**
- **Cleaning Up Afterwards**

From toasting to roasting, grilling to frying, baking to steaming, what you can't cook on a barbecue isn't worth cooking. If you're new to cookouts, why not start with grilling, the most popular and widely practised way to barbecue.

Grilling

Anything that can be cooked in 30 minutes or less is suitable for open-top grilling: steaks, chops, chicken and turkey portions, hamburgers, sausages, kebabs, whole fish and fish steaks. Remember air temperature and wind strength can greatly affect cooking time.

> **✍ Hot Tip**
> *Grilling is easy, but it does require your constant attention.*

On charcoal-burning briquettes

Having lit your fire, when most of the charcoal is covered in grey ash, it's ready for use. But before you start cooking, check the grill bars are clean and food-debris free, after which brush them with vegetable oil – or grease the griddle plate. Don't delay getting the food on the grill or griddle plate. Alternatively, you can brush the food with oil prior to placing it on the grill or griddle.

If your barbecue has an adjustable-height grill, set the level to about 8 cm (3–4 inches) above the fire-bed. Cooking at this level for a minute or so will seal in the meat juices. After searing, if possible raise the grill to 10–15 cm (4–6 inches) above the coals for the remaining cooking time.

On gas barbecues

Remove the food grill(s) before lighting the gas and brush with cooking oil. Grease the griddle pan, if using. With the lid open, ignite the gas burners at High. Close the lid and allow the barbecue's fire-bed to reach grilling heat – allow about 5–10 minutes. Replace the food grill(s) just before you start cooking.

Adjust the gas-control knobs to required setting: Low–Medium for vegetables and fruit; Medium–High for beef, pork, lamb, poultry and fish; High for searing steaks, etc., and pre-heating and cleaning. Position the food on the grill(s), generously spaced to avoid overcrowding.

Grilling tips

AVOID burning or charring meat, especially at High, by brushing on any thick basting sauce – with sugar, jam, honey or ketchup – in the final few minutes of cooking.

GRILL one side of the meat for the time recommended. Turn over to brush the uncooked surface with oil or butter and cook for the same time again to complete the cooking cycle.

MARINATE meat for a few hours, or overnight, in the refrigerator for moister, more flavoursome and tender meat when cooked. Cheaper lean cuts, such as chuck steak, benefit from an oil-based marinade.

USE long-handled tongs with 'soft jaws' to avoid piercing the meat and losing valuable juices.

THAW frozen meat while it marinates, turning it occasionally to ensure complete coverage. With time on your side, this is best done in the refrigerator.

Kebab or skewer-cooking

Meat, poultry, fish, vegetables and fruit can all be cooked on a skewer, separately or in a colourful, mouth-watering combination. For extra taste and tenderness, marinate the food first with wine, herbs and spices.

Hot Tip

For sheer versatility, skewer-cooking is tops.

Kebab tips

OIL metal skewers before threading on the food to help prevent sticking. Soak bamboo skewers in water before use to reduce the chance of them catching fire.

LEAVE the skin on fish to hold it together during cooking.

SELECT food with similar cooking times – or part-cook slower-cooking food before skewering.

USE the warming grill (rack) to support and gently cook all-vegetable kebabs as meat cooks on the grill below. Finish off the vegetables on the main grill to give them a seared look.

TRIM any excess fat to reduce potential flare-ups (see also page 48).

AVOID log jams – leave small spaces, especially between meat, to ensure even cooking.

how to cook

63

Roasts, bakes, spit-roasting and smoke-cooking: indirect-heat cooking

These are all ways of cooking by indirect heat that require a wagon or covered barbecue. Use your covered BBQ to roast joints, whole birds and thick slabs of meat as well as for fast-cooking smaller cuts of meat and hamburgers.

Roasting

On charcoal-burning barbecues

First ensure that the air-vents in the base of the barbecue are open before placing a pan in the centre of the fire-grate. Place two solid firelighters, about 10 cm (4 inches) apart, on each side of the grate. For your first indirect-heat cooking attempt, cover the firelighters with around 40 briquettes, or a good pile of natural (lumpwood) charcoal, per side. This should prove adequate for tackling a good-sized roast without having to replenish the fire. Use a long match or gas lighter to ignite the lighter blocks. When the fire-bed has become established, anywhere from 30 to 60 minutes, position the food on the grill directly above the pan. With the lid in situ, the heat from the two fire-beds will be reflected to roast or bake the food, just as your kitchen oven does.

On gas barbecues

Place a shallow steel drip pan – large enough to catch the fat but not so big that it intrudes into the lit-burner area – under the grill, to one side of the barbecue for two-burner units or in the centre of the grill for three/four-burner units. With the lid in the open position, ignite the gas burners at High, adjacent to (not under) where the drip pan is sitting.

Close the lid and leave the barbecue for 5–10 minutes. Having placed the food on the grill immediately above the drip pan, re-close the lid. Adjust the temperature setting as required (Medium should be adequate for most dishes).

> ### 🖋 Hot Tip
> *If your barbecue has limited space between the grill bars and the fire-bed, remove the rock/briquettes from the area of the grate that will remain unlit from below. Position a suitably sized steel drip pan in the vacant lot prior to igniting the adjacent burner(s).*

Baking

An apple pie or bread and butter pudding, bread or pizza can all be barbecue baked.

How to bake

The heat from the fire-bed is likely to be in an ideal state to bake a pudding or pie after a meat roast. To bake from scratch, follow the roasting directions above. Omit the drip pan, if you wish, but ensure that the charcoal fire-bed does not slip towards the centre of the grate.

Spit-roasting

Watching a leg of lamb, loin of pork, chicken or turkey revolving on a spit while relaxing in your garden with a glass of wine takes some beating. As the spit rod rotates, all the meat's surfaces are exposed to the heat, which slowly and evenly cooks the meat through without the outside burning and overcooking.

On charcoal-burning barbecues

Most charcoal barbecues (except small portables), wagon or brazier, will permit you to install a spit-roast assembly or rotisserie.

> **Hot Tip**
> *Do the spit balance test to get the best from your spit-roast: rotate the laden spit slowly across the palm of your hands. In the case of a jerky roll, re-skewer food to correct the imbalance.*

How to spit-roast First, make sure the prongs on the lower fork are facing away from the handle and then pass the spit rod through the centre of the food. For the roast to rotate smoothly, it must be evenly balanced on the spit rod. Otherwise it will rotate in fits and starts with excessive wear on the spit motor.

With a leg of lamb or pork, insert the spit into the leg at the fillet end (next to the knuckle of the leg bone) and run it carefully alongside the bone. Push a prong from the second fork into the narrow, shank end of the leg.

With a rib roast, shoulder or loin of pork, beef or lamb, insert the spit near the bones at one corner of the joint, push diagonally through the meat until it emerges close to the opposite corner.

With poultry or game, carefully push the tip of the spit through the parson's nose into the body cavity and out the neck flap. Firmly secure the forks and tie the bird into a compact shape with string.

Fill about three-quarters of the drip pan with water and add a little beer or wine and some herbs if you intend to baste with the fat-enriched liquid later in the cooking process.

how to cook

On gas barbecues

If not supplied as standard, a rotisserie can be fitted to most wagon gas barbecues. Indeed spit-roasting with the deep lid down on the largest gas wagons is highly energy efficient.

How to spit-roast Remove the food grills and place a narrow, shallow steel drip pan (or aluminium if you have a rear-mounted burner) directly on the fire-bed, parallel to, and slightly in front of, where the spit will sit. Fill with water or wine/beer/herbs if you intend to baste.

With the lid open, ignite the burners set at High. Close the lid and leave for 5–10 minutes. Turn down the heat to Medium–Low, position the food-laden spit and adjust the spit motor so that food rotates up and away from you. Adjust the drip pan so the cooking fat falls directly into it.

Spit-roasting tips

BRUSH food with oil before cooking (if not already marinated). Baste with fat/juices from the drip pan.

LEAVE a space between the meat if roasting more than one piece to allow the heat to reach all surfaces.

CHECK the level of the liquid in the drip pan periodically. Top it up now and then, but never add water where virtually all the liquid has evaporated.

Smoke-cooking

Smoke-cooking gives meat and poultry a rich colour and piquant flavour. It is not to be confused with smoke-curing, which is a preserving process for meat and fish, done at low temperatures. The prerequisite for smoke-cooking is a covered barbecue with a tight-fitting lid.

On charcoal or gas barbecues

You can smoke-cook food in any charcoal or gas-fired covered barbecue, with cooking times similar to regular barbecuing. Ham, poultry, pork (including spare ribs), lamb, venison, kidneys and sausages, and a wide range of fish and shellfish all benefit from smoke-cooking.

how to cook

On smoker barbecues

Also known as a water smoker, this is a halfway house between the traditional, ultraslow and highly skilled smoke-curing process at low temperatures and 'hot' smoking at high temperatures.

Wok-cooking

Cooking with a wok on your barbecue is a fast, healthy and fun way to prepare a wide variety of food at a modest cost. A wok and a gas barbecue constitute the ideal cooking partnership: gas is preferable to charcoal/wood because it meets the instant heat control required.

> ### 🍃 Hot Tip
> *You can use your wok not just for stir-frying but also for steaming, braising, deep- and shallow-frying.*

On charcoal-burning barbecues

Kettles and open-top brazier charcoal barbecues are your best bet, and the largest models will probably accommodate a larger wok (the larger the better). The shape and size of many charcoal-burning barbecues rule out most standard-size domestic woks, but check to see whether your barbecue will let the wok sit directly on or close to the fire-bed.

how to cook

On gas barbecues

All gas barbecues, especially those with side burners, are good for cooking with a wok.

How to wok-cook If you have a side burner, ignite it at High and place the wok squarely on the burner's trivet. Adjust the burner-control knob to the required setting after a couple of minutes.

If you have no side burner, start by removing the food grills. Ignite the burners at High, close the lid (if covered model) and leave for 5–10 minutes. Position the wok on the fire-bed, adjust the burners to the required heat and start cooking.

Wok-cooking tips

REMOVE the fire-bed (volcanic rock or ceramic briquettes) of your gas barbecue before ignition so the base of the wok sits as close as possible to the burners.

WRAP two or three layers of foil around the bottom of the wok's handle to prevent the wood from scorching.

Stir-frying tips

ALWAYS heat the wok at High for a minute or so before adding the oil.

how to cook

COAT the wok cooking surface with oil before adding any food. Any dry patches can result in sticking and burning.

DRY stir-fry ingredients as much as possible before adding them to wok to avoid splattering.

ORDER of adding the food is important – so follow the recipe.

USE cook at High – unless recipe advises otherwise.

TURN food from the bottom up.

> ### 🛩 Hot Tip
> *Before stir-frying shellfish, add a chunk of fresh ginger to the hot oil to mask the fishy aroma and enhance flavour.*

Foil cooking

Wrapping whole fish, vegetables and fruit in foil and steam-cooking them is not only healthy (they retain more of their natural colour, flavour and vitamins than when pot boiled) but also means no washing up of pots and pans later.

How to foil-cook Use heavy-duty foil or two or three layers of anything thinner. With vegetables, wrap two or three portions in foil roughly 30 cm (12 inches) square, having cleaned and prepared them first. Lift the four edges of the foil and add a tablespoon of water or olive oil or a knob of butter and season well.

How you wrap depends on whether you will be cooking via direct or indirect heat. With direct heat, you'll need to make the package as leak-proof as possible, bearing in mind that it will be turned over frequently.

> ### 🥢 Hot Tip
> *If you keep foil-wraps small, they can be easily tucked in around a roast.*

Cleaning your barbecue: gas and charcoal

After a few cookouts, your barbecue, be it gas or charcoal, will be in need of a clean, because, hygiene apart, the dirtier it gets, the less efficiently it cooks.

how to cook

Grill(s) or griddle pan

It pays dividends to get into the habit of giving the grill(s), and any griddle pan, a basic clean each time you cook. There are various tried-and-tested ways to do this.

The *wet-newspaper method* involves spreading newspaper on the ground, giving the sheets a good soaking then laying the preferably warm grill(s) on top. Cover with a few more sheets of wet newspaper. Unwrap the grill(s) a few hours later and the encrusted fat and food debris should be left behind with the newsprint.

The *wirebrush method* is good, but brushes with fine wire bristles can quickly become clogged.

The *rolled-up ball of kitchen foil method* is my preference. Crumple up a good-size piece of foil and, with a gloved hand, press it firmly down on to the warm grill bars, scrubbing along the line of bars to remove all encrusted food. Follow with a quick wipe of kitchen paper and the barbecue is ready for its next outing.

The *occasional soaking method*, in a large sink (or a shallow seed tray or some such), in a hot-water biological soap solution, should produce sparkling results.

Gas barbecues

Giving the grills and fire-bed of your covered gas barbecue a basic clean is particularly easy, and you can do it either after or before you cook.

After cooking Having removed all the food from the grill, with the barbecue still alight, close the lid and adjust all burner controls to High. Leave for 5–10 minutes, after which all fat/food residues should have burnt off the grills and out of the rocks. During the first few minutes, there will probably be a lot of smoke, so make sure you close all nearby windows and doors.

Before cooking Prior to lighting up, turn over all the cold rocks or briquettes and then add an extra minute or two to the warm-up period.

Annual spring clean To keep your barbecue in tip-top working order, treat it to an annual spring clean.

First REMOVE the grill(s), volcanic rocks or briquettes, burner and igniter assemblies. COVER the valve outlets with kitchen foil. SCRAPE and wire-brush the inside surfaces of the upper and lower housings (the lid and the casting holding the burners and supporting the grate and grills) to remove food debris. Clean off the surface with hot water and mild detergent using a scrubbing brush or scouring pad. BRUSH the surfaces of the burners with a wire brush. Clean out any clogged vents with stiff wire. REMOVE the foil from the valve outlets, clean the jet orifices (with fine wire) and replace the burner (ensuring the valve

how to cook

outlets are inside the venturi) and igniter assemblies. Replace the fire-grate and rocks or briquettes.

If the barbecue has a window in its lid, CLEAN the glass (when it is cold) using hot water and a mild cleanser. Do not use a commercial oven cleaner. CLEAN and treat any wood shelving and support structure with an approved wood preservative. CLEAN the grill(s) as described earlier. CLEAN OUT the drip pan or drip tray. TIGHTEN all the nuts and bolts in the frame assembly.

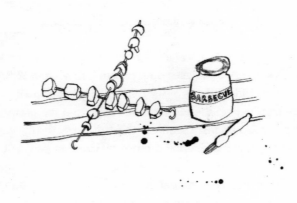

Barbecue Basics:

• Marinades, Sauces and Butters

Marinades, sauces and butters are not so much barbecue basics as essential to making the food just that bit more special. Use to add a hint of flavour or something stronger. You're halfway to a successful cookout if you marinate food first or use a sauce or butter to keep things moist, succulent and full of flavour.

MARINADES

A good marinade can promote a Championship cut of meat into Premier League material, a policy that applies to most other foods too. However, there is no substitute for quality, so buy the best you can afford (though best does not always mean most expensive).

What is a marinade?

A marinade is a seasoned liquid, in which food is steeped or tossed before cooking. Its key ingredients are acids, such as vinegar and lemon juice, oils and seasonings. Acid liquids – lemon juice, wine vinegar, wine or pineapple juice – make meat or fish more tender and enable it to absorb the flavours of any accompanying seasonings, such as herbs, spices, ginger, chilli, garlic or salt and pepper. Oil-based marinades, without acids, help to seal in any natural flavour and are primarily used to moisten the surface of fish (helping to prevent it sticking to the grill bars) or with vegetables.

How to marinate

If the marinade is acid, it's a good idea to use a glass or china dish in which to marinate. For the best results, coat the food with the marinade. If not fully covered, you will need to turn the food in the marinade from time to time. A marinade can also be used as the cooking or braising liquid.

Time and place

Successful marinating requires forward planning, but it's worth it. Some foods need only a brief encounter, say 15 minutes or so. Others benefit from more togetherness, up to 24 hours in the refrigerator – remember to remove at least an hour before cooking to allow the food to reach room temperature.

> ### 🌶 Hot Tip
> *Shake and mix food and marinade together in a strong plastic bag, seal tightly and chill.*

Basics: Marinades

With each of the starter recipes that follow, simply combine all the ingredients and mix well until blended.

Teriyaki marinade

An excellent multi-purpose marinade – good with chicken, beef, spare ribs or fish. Meat needs 4–8 hours or overnight in the refrigerator – turning occasionally; fish takes 2–4 hours. This also makes a superb basting sauce. Try it with grilled salmon steaks. *Makes about 150 ml (¼ pint).*

1½ tbsp clear honey
1½ tbsp groundnut or sunflower oil
4 tbsp dark soy sauce
1 tbsp red wine or red wine vinegar
1 tsp grated fresh root ginger
1 large garlic clove, peeled and crushed

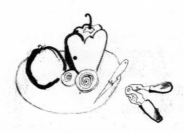

Sherry-ginger marinade

Superb for chicken, beef and spare ribs. *Makes about 150 ml (¼ pint).*

4 tbsp sweet sherry
2 tsp ground ginger
3 tbsp light soy sauce
1 tbsp fresh lemon juice
1 tbsp brown sugar
2 tbsp groundnut or sunflower oil
a few drops of Tabasco sauce, to taste
salt and freshly ground black pepper, to taste

Vegetable marinade

Particularly suitable for mixed vegetable kebabs. Allow to stand for at least an hour before use. *Makes about 150 ml (¼ pint).*

4 tbsp olive oil
150 ml (¼ pint) dry white wine
1 garlic clove, peeled and crushed
1 small red chilli, finely chopped
½ tsp dried mixed herbs
1 tsp chopped fresh mint

SAUCES

Made with good-quality ingredients, a sauce will add a luscious taste dimension to well-cooked barbecued food while protecting food against dryness during cooking.

What is a basting sauce?

A basting sauce is usually applied only after food has been partially cooked and then eaten as part of the dish. Sauces are best made in a heavy-based pan and stirred with a wooden spoon.

> #### ✐ Hot Tip
> *If fruit-based sauces, or indeed any containing sugar, are applied earlier than the remaining 10–15 minutes of cooking time, they may burn before the food is fully cooked.*

Basics: Sauces

A selection of sauces – for meat, fish and veg.

Jim's universal sauce

Great served with chicken, pork, beef or fish. The recipe makes enough for future home cookouts, but why not bottle up any extra and take it along to your next away cookout. *Makes about 1.2 litres (2 pints).*

2 tbsp groundnut oil
2 garlic cloves, peeled and crushed
2 small green peppers, seeded and finely chopped
2 small onions, peeled and finely chopped
125 g (4 oz) celery, finely chopped
½ tsp dried basil
½ tsp dried thyme
½ tsp ground cinnamon
1 tsp salt
2 dashes Tabasco sauce
½ tbsp Worcestershire sauce
450 ml (¾ pint) tomato ketchup
6 tbsp red or white wine vinegar
1 lemon, juiced, plus 1 tsp grated zest

Heat the oil in a large, heavy-based pan and add the garlic, peppers, onions and celery. Cook over a medium heat for about 5 minutes, stirring frequently. Add 300 ml (½ pint) water and all the remaining ingredients except the lemon juice and zest, and cook for a further 5 minutes. Add the lemon juice and zest, and simmer over a gentle heat for 30–40 minutes, stirring occasionally. Add a little more water if the sauce is too thick.

Lily's luxury tomato sauce

Served warm or cold with hamburgers, sausages, steak, chops and fish, you'll find this versatile sauce goes with pretty much anything. *Makes about 250 ml (8 fl oz).*

1 tbsp extra-virgin olive oil
15 g (½ oz) butter
1 medium onion, peeled and finely chopped
1 garlic clove, peeled and crushed
1 tsp dried mixed herbs
2 large ripe tomatoes, skinned and roughly chopped
125 ml (4 fl oz) tomato purée
2 tsp balsamic vinegar
salt and freshly ground black pepper, to taste

Heat the oil and butter in a heavy-based pan and add the onion, garlic and herbs. Cook for 3 minutes or until the onion has softened. Stir in the tomatoes, tomato purée and vinegar and cook for a further 4–5 minutes, stirring occasionally. Remove the pan from the heat and allow to cool. Liquidise the sauce in a food processor until smooth. Season to taste.

BUTTERS

A flavoured butter makes food such as lean meat more succulent and helps to protect it from dryness when cooked at a high heat.

Thinking ahead

Flavoured butter can be made 7–10 days in advance and stored in a covered dish in the refrigerator.

How to use

You can melt the butter and brush it on to the food, or put a small knob on top during the final two minutes of cooking and allow it to melt down. Some of the butters make tasty and economical sandwich spreads.

All flavoured butters are suitable for freezing, so make it easy for yourself and make ahead.

Basics: Butters

A moment's blending creates some brilliant butters for all foods.

Preparation

Beat the butter until soft then thoroughly mix in the remaining ingredients. Using wet hands, shape the butter into a roll about 4 cm (1½ inches) in diameter. Wrap gently in foil and chill well. Keep in the refrigerator until ready to serve.

Garlic butter

A perennial favourite – goes with most things, especially red meat, seafood, veg and, of course, French bread. This one's medium strength, so add more garlic, as you prefer.

1 garlic clove, peeled and finely chopped
1½ tbsp chopped fresh flatleaf parsley
125 g (4 oz) butter

Lime and dill butter

Slither over seafood, poultry and vegetables.

1 tsp freshly grated lime zest
2 tsp fresh lime juice
½ tsp finely chopped fresh dill
¼ tsp grated fresh root ginger
125 g (4 oz) butter

Tarragon and parsley butter

A match for red meat, especially steaks.

¼ tsp crushed dried tarragon
1 tbsp finely chopped fresh flatleaf parsley
½ tsp grated lemon zest
2 tsp fresh lemon juice
¼ tsp salt
125 g (4 oz) butter

barbecue basics

Barbecue Basics: Fish and Shellfish

- **Which Fish and Shellfish Barbecues Best?**
- **How to Barbecue Fish and Shellfish Successfully**
- **Recipe Essentials**

Like love and marriage or horse and carriage, there are some recipes that just go with barbecue cookouts. Consider these your barbecue basics: easy to prepare and cook, delicious to eat, soon to become firm favourites. Let's start with fish and shellfish.

Barbecuing fish

When it comes to choosing what to barbecue, fish-wise, the world is your oyster. Sardine, herring, mackerel, trout, snapper, sea bass or red mullet and meaty-textured, firm fish such as tuna and salmon steak, cod, monkfish, swordfish, halibut, turbot or squid all barbecue brilliantly. You can also griddle fish cakes.

Barbecuing shellfish

Prawns, scallops, lobster, mussels and oysters are perfect for cooking on the grill. There are a few simple crustacean ground rules to follow. Cook in the shell whenever possible to preserve liquid and flavour. Work quickly at Medium–High, and avoid overcooking – it's a sin.

Hot Tip

Defrost frozen meat, fish or shellfish in the refrigerator or microwave – not at room temperature. Bacteria can grow in outer thawing flesh while the inside is still defrosting.

Tips for cooking fish and shellfish

The big bonus with fish and shellfish is that generally it's quick to cook. But the downside is that you'll need to keep an eye on it to avoid over cooking. And, while grilling fish is a simple cooking technique, practise makes perfect.

Always bear in mind that fish will carry on gently cooking after it is removed from the grill.

Too much flipping can cause fish to fall apart – it seems to like nothing more than to stick to grill bars and baskets and it can be delicate. So keep turning to a minimum.

Foil wrapping is useful. But, if you want the full barbecue flavour – unless you are grilling fragile fillets – cook directly on the fire or, for large, whole fish, by indirect heat. Just brush with oil to avoid sticking.

Or, to keep fish and shellfish succulent on the grill, you can wrap them in a green vine leaf or a lettuce leaf.

Tuna, salmon and other firm fish can be cooked directly on the grill if you handle it with care. Consider investing in a hinged wire basket or holder for fragile fish or shellfish.

Avoid overcooking: fish is cooked when no longer translucent but slightly opaque throughout. An easy way to test if it's ready is to probe into the thickest part of the fish with a thin metal or bamboo skewer – as the fish cooks the firmness of flesh will relax to the point where the skewer will meet little resistance.

Basics: Recipes

To whet your appetite – and have a go at grilling, wok- and skewer-cooking as well as baking a whole fish.

Szechuan prawns

Try out your wok with these spicy prawns. *Serves 2.*

500 g (1 lb) raw tiger prawns, shells intact, veined and legs removed
2 tbsp groundnut oil

For the marinade
2 spring onions, roughly chopped
2 x 2.5 cm (1 inch) pieces fresh root ginger, peeled and crushed
50 g (2 oz) mangetout or French beans, cut into 5 cm (2 inch) lengths
½ tsp sesame oil
3 tbsp rice wine or dry sherry
1 tsp sugar
6 tbsp soy sauce
1 dried red chilli, seeded and crushed

Combine all the marinade ingredients in a bowl. Add the prawns, stir and cover with cling film. Marinate in the refrigerator for 2–3 hours, stirring occasionally. Remove the prawns from the marinade, drain,

barbecue basics: fish and shellfish

reserving the marinade, and pat dry with kitchen paper. Add the groundnut oil to the hot wok. When the oil is hot, add the prawns and stir-fry at High for 3–4 minutes. The prawns are done when they turn pink. Add the reserved marinade to the prawns, bring to the boil then serve immediately.

Sardines with herb and garlic butter

Grilling an oily fish, such as these fresh sardines, is ideal barbecue fare. *Serves 4.*

20 small fresh sardines, cleaned
4 tbsp olive oil
salt and freshly ground black pepper

Herb and garlic butter
½ tsp dried tarragon or rosemary
1 tbsp finely chopped fresh chives
1 tbsp finely chopped fresh flatleaf parsley
1 garlic clove, peeled and finely chopped
¼ tsp salt + pinch of freshly ground black pepper
125 g (4 oz) butter, beaten till soft

Brush the sardines lightly with the oil and season to taste with salt and pepper. Grill at High for about 3–4 minutes each side. Add the herbs and seasoning to the butter and serve with the fish.

Mushroom and scallop kebabs

Skewer-cooking is perfect for these lovely buttery kebabs. *Serves 2*.

12 large scallops
12 closed-cap or large button mushrooms,
   stalks removed
6 tbsp melted butter
juice of 1 lemon
salt and freshly ground black pepper, to taste

Place a scallop in each mushroom and spike on a pre-soaked bamboo skewer. Use three scallops and mushrooms per skewer, leaving a 2.5 cm (1 inch) gap between each of them. Mix the lemon juice into the melted butter and brush generously over the kebabs. Season lightly with salt and pepper. Grill at Medium for about 8 minutes, turning and basting frequently. The scallops are cooked when they have just turned opaque and are slightly firm to the touch. Pour any remaining butter into a bowl and serve with the kebabs.

Baked whole fish

This is particularly suitable for sea bass, salmon and red mullet, especially when cooked in a wire fish holder – large ones are available – and it is the ideal accessory when grilling directly over a fire-bed, charcoal or gas. You can also bake the fish in a greased roasting tin or foil pan. *Serves 6–12.*

1 whole fish, about 1.75–3 kg (4–7 lb), cleaned and scaled

For the marinade
4 spring onions, finely chopped
1 tsp salt
1 tsp sugar
1 tsp grated fresh root ginger
1 tbsp dark soy sauce
1 tbsp sake, dry sherry or wine
1 tbsp groundnut oil or 2 tsp sesame oil, plus extra for brushing

Score the fish, almost to the bone, with three parallel diagonal slashes on each side. Combine the marinade ingredients. Rub the fish with the marinade, inside and out, and chill for 30 minutes. If you're grilling directly over the fire-bed, brush the inside of the fish holder with oil first. Grill the fish at Medium–High, allowing 10 minutes for every 2.5 cm (1 inch) thickness and carefully turning midway through, brushing with oil before you do so. When baking by indirect heat, increase the time to 12–13 minutes per similar thickness. The fish is ready when the skin is nicely browned and probing with a metal or bamboo skewer meets little resistance.

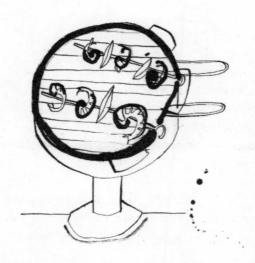

Barbecue Basics: Meat

- **Best Cuts: Quick and Slow**
- **How to Barbecue Meat Successfully**
- **Basic Recipes: Beef, Lamb, Pork and Poultry**

If you think bangers and burgers are all there is to barbecuing meat, you'll be pleased to know that you can barbecue virtually all cuts of meat – with great success and little effort.

Barbecuing meat

All meat is good for barbecuing. However, good results start with the selection of a prime lean cut that will stand up to direct heat from the fire-bed and brown evenly without becoming tough. The meat should lie reasonably flat on the grill, which makes all the prime beef steaks and chops of lamb and pork great candidates for direct grilling. Less obvious choices, but equally suitable, are boned leg, and shoulder, of lamb and boned loin of pork. The field widens when you cut up small pieces of the various meats for skewer-cooking. Large, irregularly shaped cuts, such as leg of lamb or pork and loin of venison, are ideal for spit-roasting.

If you're in a hurry, go for minced meat – easy to prepare in single servings and quick to cook. The favourite technique, beloved by all, is to mould gently (go easy on the squeeze) into hamburger shapes. They should be at least 2.5cm (1 inch) thick but make sure they are cooked all the way through. Alternatively, shape the mince into a smooth cylinder round a flat-bladed skewer. If time is not an issue, you can do wonders in terms of succulence and flavour by cooking large joints of meat in a smoker barbecue over a period of 5–6 hours or more.

🔥 Hot Tip

Take some stress out of party cooking by part-cooking meat, such as ribs or turkey legs, indoors and then giving them a final flavoursome blast on the barbecue.

Tips for cooking meat

Go for prime cuts with plenty of marbling that melts during grilling to help keep the meat moist.

Use a marinade: the acid in a marinade, either wine, wine vinegar, fruit juice, cider or beer, acts as a tenderising/flavouring agent, while oil helps to moisten very lean meat.

Pierce or slash thicker, denser cuts to help the marinade permeate well into the meat.

Avoid any hint of pink in pork, chicken, sausages, burgers and minced meat, etc., to avoid the possibility of food poisoning.

Meat on the bone makes chops, chicken drumsticks, spare ribs easier to handle. With the added bonus that the bone helps to conduct heat, ensuring faster cooking and safer eating.

Good joints for barbecuing are legs of lamb and pork, rib of beef and gammon.

Popular for a reason: sausages and burgers are perfect barbecue fast food.

Basics: Recipes

BEEF

From beef burgers to roast beef, red meat and barbecues are a match made in heaven. Of course, venison is a good red meat for barbecuing too.

Chuck-wagon hamburgers

A classic stretched burger recipe that smells as yummy as it tastes and will get you in the mood for outdoor cookouts – no barbecue is complete without a burger. *Serves 6.*

1 small onion, peeled and finely chopped
1 green pepper, seeded and finely chopped
2 medium carrots, peeled and grated
1 garlic clove, peeled and crushed
500 g (1 lb) chuck steak, finely minced
2 tsp Worcestershire sauce
3 tbsp vegetable oil
50 g (2 oz) fresh white breadcrumbs
1 tsp salt
1 tsp freshly ground black pepper
1 egg, lightly beaten
6 soft rolls, toasted, to serve
2 large tomatoes, sliced, to garnish

Sauté the onion, green pepper, carrot and garlic in a pan until softened and drain well on kitchen paper. In a large bowl, lightly but thoroughly mix the sautéed veg with the steak, Worcestershire sauce, oil, breadcrumbs and salt and pepper. Bind the mixture with the beaten egg and shape into six burgers approximately 2 cm (¾ inch) thick. Cook on the grill or griddle plate at Medium–High for about 8–10 minutes on each side till cooked through and piping hot. Toast the cut side of the rolls on the grill, and top each burger with a tomato slice to serve.

Quick-fried beef with Chinese leaves

Quite a stirring little recipe, for quick and easy wok cooking. *Serves 4.*

> **500 g (1 lb) fillet or rump steak, sliced into 5–6 cm**
>   **(2–2½ inch) strips**
> **4 tbsp vegetable oil**
> **750 g (1½ lb) Chinese lettuce, leaves cut into 5 cm**
>   **(2 inch) strips**
> **salt and freshly ground black pepper, to taste**
> **3 tsp cornflour**
> **3 tbsp oyster sauce**
> **1 tsp sesame oil**
> **½ tsp sugar**
> **2 tbsp cold water**

For the marinade
1 tsp sake or dry sherry
1 tsp dark soy sauce
½ tsp sugar
1 tsp sesame oil
1 medium egg yolk

In a bowl, combine all the marinade ingredients and add the beef strips. Leave to marinate in a cool place for about 1 hour. Heat two tablespoons of the vegetable oil in the wok. Add the Chinese leaves and stir-fry at High until tender. Season the leaves and arrange over a large platter. Drain the beef strips, sprinkle with the cornflour and mix. Heat the remaining vegetable oil in the wok and stir-fry the beef until golden brown. Remove the beef and keep warm. Add the oyster sauce to the wok and when it begins to bubble, return the beef to the wok along with the sesame oil, sugar and water. Keep stirring until the sauce thickens and the beef is heated through. Serve the beef scattered over the Chinese leaves.

LAMB

When it comes to barbecuing lamb, the mince is good for burgers, chops or leg steaks ideal for grilling and you can roast or spit-roast a shoulder or leg of lamb.

Greek lamb kebabs

Just shut your eyes and you'll think you're in Greece. Terrific served with a tomato salad. *Serves 4.*

> **750 g (1½ lb) lamb leg shanks, trimmed and cut into 2 cm (¾ inch) cubes**
> **salt and freshly ground black pepper**
> **1 tsp dried marjoram or 1 tbsp chopped fresh marjoram**
> **2 small onions, peeled and quartered**
> **4 tbsp olive, plus extra for greasing**
> **1 tbsp fresh lemon juice**
> **8 bay leaves**
> **lemon wedges, for garnishing**

Put the lamb cubes in a dish and season with the salt, pepper and marjoram. Split the onions into layers and set the thick outer layers on top of the seasoned lamb. Reserve the inner layers. Add the oil and lemon juice to the lamb mixture and stir well. Cover the dish with cling film and leave to chill for 3–4 hours. Divide the cubes of lamb among 4 oiled metal skewers, with a thin onion slice and half a bay leaf between every second cube of meat. Grill the kebabs at Medium for about 10–15 minutes, depending on how well done you like your lamb. Turn the kebabs several times during cooking. Serve garnished with the lemon wedges.

🔥 Hot Tip

For an extra special touch with lamb kebabs, replace the metal skewers with sharpened twigs from a mature rosemary bush, leaving some leaves at the unsharpened end for a great aroma during cooking and great presentation.

barbecue basics: meat

Leg of lamb with anchovies, garlic and rosemary

Spit-roasting lamb is much easier than you might think – and perfect for Sunday lunch. *Serves 8–10.*

2.25–2.75 kg (5–6 lb) leg of lamb
4 garlic cloves, peeled and cut lengthways into 3 slivers
2 x 50 g cans anchovies in oil, drained
12 small sprigs fresh rosemary
75 g (3 oz) unsalted butter, softened
juice of 1 lemon
freshly ground black pepper

Make 12 deep incisions in the fleshy side of the joint with a sharp, narrow-blade knife. Insert a garlic slice, half an anchovy and a sprig of rosemary into each cut. Cream the remaining anchovies with the butter and lemon juice and spread the mixture over the joint. Grind pepper over the buttered meat. Spit-roast at Medium, basting once or twice with some of the juices from the drip pan. If you like your meat slightly pink in the centre (fine for lamb), cook for about 1¼–1½ hours or until the meat thermometer reads 60–65°C (140–150°F). A reading of 71°C (160°F) indicates medium, while 77°C (170°F) is well done. Remove the joint from the spit, cover with foil and leave to rest for 15–20 minutes before carving.

PORK

The other white meat, pork is extremely versatile and perfect for barbecues: from gammon, bacon and ham to ribs, fillets, leg and loin.

Pork and apple burgers

You can't have too many burger recipes for a cookout – the pork and apple combine well to make this one of my favourites. *Serves 6.*

>   1 kg (2 lb) lean minced pork
>   1 medium apple, finely chopped
>   1 egg, beaten
>   75 g (3 oz) fresh white breadcrumbs
>   1 tsp garlic salt
>   ¼ tsp onion salt
>   ¼ tsp freshly ground black pepper
>   2 tbsp olive oil
>   6 hamburger buns, halved

Mix together the pork, apple, egg and enough of the breadcrumbs to give a firm, not too wet, mixture. Shape carefully into six burgers. Blend the garlic salt and onion salt, pepper and oil and brush some of the

barbecue basics: meat

mixture on one side of the burgers. Grill the oiled side of the burgers, or cook on a griddle plate, over Medium–High for about 10 minutes. Brush the burgers with the rest of the oil mixture, turn and cook on the other side for a further 10 minutes or until nicely browned. Toast the buns during the last few minutes of cooking time. Serve with your favourite barbecue sauce.

Stir-fried pork with oyster sauce

Stir-frying is like a dance – slow, quick, quick, slow. The first slow step is the patient food preparation before heating the wok. *Serves 4.*

250 g (8 oz) lean pork, preferably tenderloin, sliced into bite-size pieces
3 tbsp vegetable oil
250 g (8 oz) spinach, torn into 5 cm (2 in) strips
½ tsp salt
¼ tsp sugar
2 tbsp oyster sauce
6 baby sweetcorn, snapped into small pieces
½ tsp sesame oil
freshly ground black pepper

For the marinade
½ tsp light soy sauce
½ tsp sesame oil
1 tsp rice wine or dry sherry
½ tsp sugar
1 egg yolk
1 tbsp cornflour
salt and freshly ground black pepper, to taste

Combine the marinade ingredients, apart from the cornflour, in a bowl, add the pork pieces and marinate for about 10 minutes. Heat one tablespoon of the vegetable oil in the wok. Add the spinach and the salt and stir-fry quickly at High. Add the sugar and one tablespoon of water and stir again. Drain the liquid from the wok, remove the spinach and keep warm. Heat the remaining vegetable oil in the wok. Stir the cornflour into the marinating pork and stir-fry in the wok at High until golden brown all over. Remove the pork from the wok and keep warm. Add the oyster sauce to the wok and when it starts to bubble add the pork again and stir-fry for about 1 minute. Add the cooked spinach and the sweetcorn, sprinkle with the sesame oil and a grinding of black pepper and stir-fry for another minute or so. Serve immediately.

POULTRY

Chicken, and other poultry such as duck or turkey, and game birds such as quail and guinea fowl, are all suitable for the barbecue, be they drumsticks or thighs, wings or breasts; stir fries, grills or griddles. You can roast whole birds too.

Streaky drumsticks

Everyone loves a chicken drumstick – they cook quickly and at roughly the same time, and the dark meat is flavoursome and ideal finger food. *Serves 4.*

> **8 plump chicken drumsticks**
> **75 g (3 oz) soft medium-fat cheese**
> **salt and freshly ground black pepper**
> **8 rashers rindless unsmoked streaky bacon**
> **groundnut or sunflower oil, for basting**
> **8 wooden cocktail sticks, soaked in water**

Make deep cuts in the fattest part of each drumstick and fill each slit with the soft cheese. Season with salt and pepper, then wrap a bacon rasher around each drumstick and secure with a cocktail stick. Grill at

Medium–High, basting frequently with oil, for about 12 minutes on each side or until cooked.

Chicken Teriyaki

Chicken wings are another barbecue basic – either roasted, as here, or grilled, in which case reduce the cooking time by about 15 minute and baste the chicken occasionally with some of the reserved marinade. *Makes 20.*

20 meaty chicken wings

For the teriyaki marinade: see page 77

Cut through the wing joints and discard the pointed tips. Carefully loosen the flesh around the lower joints of the wings with a small sharp knife and push down both flesh and skin so they resemble mini-lollipops. In a bowl, mix all the ingredients for the marinade and add the chicken. Cover with cling film and chill for 2–3 hours or overnight in a refrigerator, turning the chicken occasionally. Drain the chicken and reserve the marinade. Cook, basting frequently, with the lid down at Medium–High for 20–30 minutes or until cooked and turned a dark golden-mahogany.

Hot Tip
Use any discarded pointed chicken wing tips for grilling as
appetiser titbits – the chook equivalent of pork scratchings.

Barbecue Basics: Veg and Fruit

- **Which Veg and Fruit Barbecues Best?**
- **How to Barbecue Fruit and Vegetables Successfully**
- **Recipe Essentials**

Barbecuing does for vegetables what English mustard does for roast beef – it enhances their flavour in a big way. As a meal in themselves or a side dish to the main meaty event, vegetables are versatile barbecue food – a great alternative to salad, which always works well with barbecued meat and fish.

If you are entertaining non-meat eaters, they won't feel cheated by what's available. And, of course, while desserts are not always a cookout priority, barbecued fruit is scrumptious as well as easy and fun to cook – a barbecue bonus.

VEGETABLES

A variety of vegetables are delicious cooked on the barbecue, either grilled, baked wrapped in foil to steam (broccoli, runner and broad beans, asparagus spears, peas and Brussels sprouts lend themselves to this) or nestled amid the glowing coals. Root vegetables, such as potatoes and parsnips, yams, carrots and beetroot, all barbecue well. Sweetcorn is the veg equivalent of the sausage, a perennial favourite, good as finger food. Skewer cooking allows you to cook a wide selection of veg, from courgettes, aubergines, mushrooms and tomatoes to peppers, onions and new potatoes, as one delicious dish.

Tips for barbecuing vegetables

Set aside a section of the grill for vegetables in case you are cooking for vegetarians: this avoids contact with uncooked meat.

Marinating is good for flavour and to avoid drying out – experiment with your favourite herbs and oils and see the Vegetable marinade on page 78.

Avoid overcooking or you'll end up with rubbery or wrinkly dried-out veg.

Don't cook the veg too soon – if you leave it waiting while the meat cooks, it will wilt and look and taste unappealing.

Odds are that at least one of your party guests will be vegetarian. If this is the case, grill some tasty burgers, made with either Quorn or tofu, to accompany their veg.

Bear in mind when grilling different veg together that the timing must be orchestrated. Slow-cookers first and fast-cooking ones added last.

BASIC VEG

What could be easier than popping a baking potato, pricked all over with a fork and brushed with oil, on the barbecue (either wrapped in foil – or not if you prefer a crispy skin)? Served on its own with, say, seasoned butter or your own choice of topping, there's little to beat it. Other veg can be just as simple.

Sweetcorn with dill

For good reason, sweetcorn is a traditional barbecue vegetable – here with a herby twist. You could leave out the herbs and smear the corn with garlic butter (see page 83) and grill wrapped with streaky bacon as an alternative for dedicated meat eaters. *Serves 6.*

6 young sweetcorn cobs, in their husks
125 g (4 oz) butter, softened
1 tsp fresh dill
6 coriander seeds, crushed
1 tsp salt
a pinch of grated fresh nutmeg

Loosen the husks enough to strip away the silk. Soak the cobs in iced water for at least 30 minutes. Blend the remaining ingredients and gently peel back but preserve the husks to spread the seasoned butter generously over the well-drained sweetcorn. Re-site the husks and place each cob on a sheet of foil and wrap securely. Grill at Medium for 15–20 minutes, turning several times.

 Hot Tip
Leaving potatoes in their skins adds to their flavour.

Potato kebabs madras
One of my favourite potato dishes – with great eye appeal. You can ring the changes with different curry powder/paste. *Serves 4.*

750 g (1½ lb) new or main-crop potatoes, washed and cut
    into 2.5–4 cm (1–1½ inch) cubes
6 tbsp curry paste or powder, blended with 2–3 tbsp water
oil, for greasing
salt

Cook the potato cubes in boiling, salted water, until barely tender but not overcooked.

Drain thoroughly and cool. Thread the cubes on to oiled metal (preferably flat-bladed) skewers, leaving a small gap between each cube. Generously brush the cubes with the curry paste or powder and allow to stand for up to 1 hour. Grill at High for about 10 minutes or until the potato cubes are uniformly cooked on all sides. Baste once or twice during cooking with any leftover paste. Serve immediately.

Gem squash McTaggart

You can use other squash here too, such as butternut – and either grill or bake. *Serves 1–2.*

> **1 gem squash, stem removed, cut in half and seeded**
> **50 g (2 oz) butter**
> **salt and freshly ground black pepper**

Divide the butter between the inside of the halves. Season lightly with salt and a generous grinding of pepper. Place each half in the centre of a square of heavy-duty kitchen foil roughly three times the diameter of the squash. Fold the four corners over the veg into a pyramid shape. Loosely seal the edges. Keep upright and, at High, either grill for about 15 minutes, or bake for 25–30 minutes.

FOR VEGETARIANS

With non-meat eaters in mind, but good for everyone else too.

Halloumi with lemon and garlic

A tasty appetiser that hints at Mediterranean sunshine. *Serves 4.*

1 block halloumi cheese, cut into 8 even slices

For the lemon and garlic vinaigrette
1 tbsp fresh lemon juice
1 garlic clove, finely chopped
1 tsp freshly ground black pepper
1 rounded tsp mustard powder
1 tbsp chopped fresh coriander leaves
3 tbsp extra-virgin olive oil

In a small bowl, whisk together the vinaigrette ingredients. Grill the cheese slices at Medium–High for about 1 minute on each side or until light golden – avoid rubbery cheese by not overcooking. Cut the cheese into strips and serve immediately with the vinaigrette poured over and some bread to soak it up.

Mixed vegetable kebabs

The different vegetables create a brilliant blend of flavours. *Serves 6.*

6 tiny potatoes, preferably new
6 small onions or shallots
12 small closed-cap mushrooms, stalks removed
1 large green pepper, seeded and cut into 6 pieces
2 small courgettes, cut into 6 pieces, 2.5–4 cm
  (1–1½ inches) long
50 g (2 oz) butter, melted
½ tsp garlic salt
¼ tsp freshly ground black pepper
6 tiny firm tomatoes
oil, for greasing

Boil the potatoes and onions separately in lightly salted water until they are barely tender. Drain and thread all but the tomatoes alternately on to six oiled metal (preferably flat-bladed) skewers. Blend the melted butter, garlic salt and pepper and brush generously over the kebabs. Grill at Medium–High for about 5 minutes, turning and basting frequently, and adding a tomato to each skewer for a final 5 minutes' cooking time.

Ratatouille

This goes down well with chicken, lamb, beef or fish, or just by itself.
Serves 4–6.

6 tbsp olive oil
2 large onions, peeled and thinly sliced
3 garlic cloves, peeled and crushed
1 medium aubergine, thinly sliced
1 medium red pepper, seeded and roughly chopped
1 medium green pepper, seeded and roughly chopped
4 small courgettes, thinly sliced
2 large tomatoes, skinned, seeded and cut into wedges
1 tbsp chopped fresh basil
1 tsp dried rosemary
1 bay leaf
1 tsp salt
½ tsp freshly ground black pepper
2 tbsp chopped fresh flatleaf parsley

Heat the oil at High in a large frying pan or roasting tin. Add the onion and garlic and cook for about 5 minutes or until the onions are soft and translucent. Add the aubergine, peppers and courgettes and cook for a further 5 minutes, frequently shaking the frying pan or stirring the tin. Add the tomatoes and herbs, except the parsley, and seasoning. Sprinkle over the parsley. Reduce the heat to Medium if cooking with gas or reposition frying pan/tin to a cooler spot. Cook for a further 50–60 minutes. Serve hot or cold.

FRUIT

Barbecuing fruit

You can simply barbecue bananas in their skins, or take the stone out of a peach or nectarine and sprinkle the halves with sugar or drizzle with brandy or honey before cooking. Sliced pineapple or apples, pears and grapefruit are all suitable for grilling. Skewer-cooked fruit kebabs are a favourite. You can serve fruit with some meats too, such as peaches with ham, pork or poultry.

Tips for barbecuing fruit

Section off part of the grill for fruit: this avoids contact with uncooked meat, etc.

Make the most of some of the firmer fruits, such as apples, pears and melon, mango, grapes and pineapple, by marinating them first.

Try an alcohol or honey/sugar-based syrup as a marinade so that the fruit caramelises as it cooks.

Prepare fruit in advance and leave it to cook slowly once the other courses are done.

Skewer-cook the firmer fruits; foil-wrap soft fruits.

Ensure an unlimited supply of ice cream, cream or yoghurt – the perfect cold accompaniment to hot barbecued fruit.

BASIC FRUIT

This is the one basic fruit recipe that has stood me in good stead over the years as a desirable dessert at many a barbecue.

Mixed fruit and bread kebabs

A barbecue special – these will just fly off the plate. *Serves 6.*

2 firm ripe pears, peeled, cored and cut into large chunks
1 small melon, peeled and chopped into bite-size pieces
2 oranges, cut into 1 cm (½ inch) slices, each then quartered
1 small pineapple, peeled and cored, cut into 2.5 cm (1 inch)
    pieces, or 250 g can pineapple chunks
12 large firm strawberries
2 medium firm bananas, each peeled and cut into 3 chunks
6 large seedless grapes
juice of 2 lemons
125 g (4 oz) caster sugar, plus extra for dusting
3 tbsp liqueur, choose your favourite
4 tbsp white wine
1 white loaf, crusts removed, sliced into 2.5 cm (1 inch) cubes
125 g (4 oz) butter, melted
oil, for greasing

Put all the fruit in a large bowl with the lemon juice and half the sugar, the liqueur and the wine. Mix gently together with your hands and leave to chill for 20–30 minutes. Brush the bread cubes with the melted butter and toss in a separate bowl with the remaining sugar. Divide a selection of fruit, plus two pieces of bread, among six oiled metal skewers, preferably flat-bladed, reserving the marinade. Grill at Medium for about 5 minutes, turning and dusting with more sugar, until the kebabs are lightly caramelised. Warm any remaining marinade and pour over the kebabs before serving, if you wish.

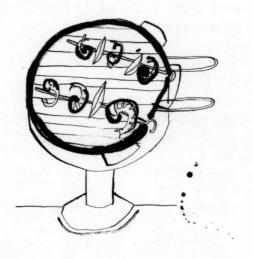

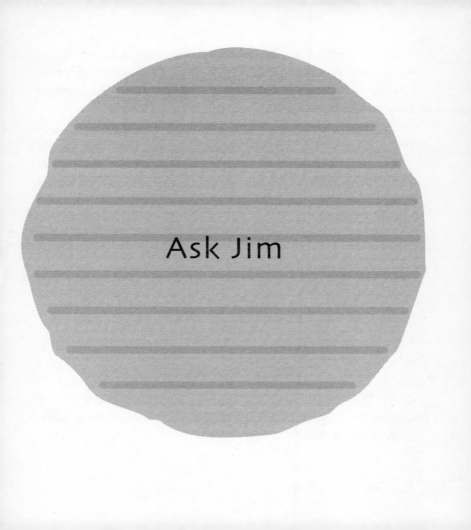

Ask Jim

I have been professionally involved in the barbecue business for almost four decades, and teaching the tricks of the trade for almost as long, so I should have got the hang of it by now. Here are a few of the questions I often get asked – you might like to learn from my hard-earned experience.

Q: I always brush oil generously over the food grill of my barbecue before cooking. Despite this, flat items, such as chops and steaks, invariably stick to the grill bars, making it difficult to turn the meat over. How can I prevent this?

A: This problem can occur when the oil is applied to a grill sitting over a very hot fire. If you're not quick, the oil burns off almost immediately, which results in you placing the food on a dry grill. Although I used to advocate pre-oiling the grill, I now prefer lightly spraying or brushing the food with oil pre-cooking.

> 🪶 **Hot Tip**
> *Oil the food, not the grill.*

Q: My long wooden-handled skewers are impossible to fit into even the largest roasting tin when I want to marinate kebabs. Any suggestions?

A: Think vertically. How about using a tall jug or even a vase? This should enable you to accommodate, and twirl, several laden skewers at a time.

Q: Is there an easy way to judge the temperature of my charcoal fire-bed?

A: When most of the coals are covered in grey ash, carefully position your hand, fingers extended and palm down, about 2.5 cm (1 inch) above the food grill. Count how many seconds you can hold it there before the fire-bed heat forces you to move your hand away: 2 seconds: Hot. 3 seconds: Medium/Hot. 4 seconds: Medium. 5 seconds: Low.

Q: If you had to give just three tips to anyone using a charcoal barbecue for the first time, what would they be?

A: 1 Light the prepared fire-bed 35–40 minutes before you need to start cooking. 2 Never allow yourself to be coerced into starting to cook until you are happy with the temperature of the fire-bed – you could end up with undercooked food and even more impatient and hungry guests. 3 During the hectic pre-party preparation period

carry in your apron pocket a kitchen timer or your mobile phone.
Set it to remind you when to put a match to your prepared fire-bed.
Re-set it for another 30 minutes or so once you've lit the fire-bed so
you remember to check to see if it is ready for cooking.

🖋 Hot Tip

*For stress-free success, light your barbecue well in advance
of when you want to cook.*

Q: **I am planning a 'Spare-rib Spectacular' barbecue party for
family and friends. I only have two medium-size gas
barbecues on which to cook several dozen ribs. Knowing that
a meaty rib takes over an hour to cook, I am in a quandary
how to cope.**

A: A few hours before party time, place the marinated slabs of ribs,
meaty side up, in shallow roasting tins. Cook, uncovered, in a
Medium–Hot oven for just over an hour, basting frequently with any
reserved marinade. Drain off the excess fat, cover with foil and keep
cool until your barbecues are ready. Finish cooking the ribs on the
barbecue for 10–20 minutes or until well browned and crisp. Carve
into individual ribs and serve.

Q: I am organising a large charity-fundraising barbecue: how should I cater for it so that not only is there enough food for everyone but also no wasteful excess. Is there a formula to which I can work?

A: A barbecue is a moving feast in that people tend to perambulate, thus apparently stimulating the appetite. They also seem to eat more when they eat outside. To be on the safe side you might like to increase your non-veg shopping list by a factor of 1½–2 with a 10 per cent back-up of staple items such as sausages and burgers. As a rough guide reckon on 170–225g (6–8 oz) of boneless lean meat (including burgers, sausages and kebabs) per adult. You should increase by half the weight allowance per head if serving only meat on the bone, such as spare ribs or chops. Overstocking can turn out to be a plus rather than a minus when guests, who swore they couldn't eat another thing at 8 p.m., have become ravenous again by around 10.45 p.m.

Q: After years of constant use, my trusty old charcoal-burning barbecue is on its last legs. Do I buy another charcoal unit or, like most of my friends, go for gas?

ask jim

A: It is likely that some of your friends have faced this dilemma, so why not ask them: charcoal or gas? To a large extent, your choice is about whether you enjoy building a charcoal fire (a primal experience) or simply prefer ignition at the push of a button, knowing that, in all likelihood, you will be cooking those steaks in just 10 minutes.

Is cost an issue? Although initially more expensive, gas barbecues cost less to operate in the medium-to-long term. Taste-wise, tests indicate no significant flavour difference. Gas barbecues are easier to light and control heat-wise. So, will the practical benefits make you more likely to barbecue at the drop of a hat? Everything considered, it's a lifestyle choice. Like many people I have a foot in both camps, which suits me well.

Q: How do I know if the steaks or chops I am grilling are cooked to the required rare, medium or well done?

A: Professional chefs and experienced cooks use their eyes – and an index finger pressed into the surface of the meat. The way a piece of meat feels is a strong indicator of how well it is done. Here's how:

Step 1 Let one of your hands dangle limply from the wrist. Gently push the tip of the index finger of the other hand into the ball of the fully relaxed thumb. The resistance you feel should be similar to prodding a *rare* steak.

Step 2 Straighten the hand and push the tip of the index finger into the ball of the thumb. The resistance should roughly equate to a *medium* steak.

Step 3 Fully stretch and straighten your hand. The resistance should roughly equate to a *well done* steak. But, rather than using my index finger I use the closed jaws of a pair of tongs or the bottom side of the tines of a long-handled fork.

Q: The volcanic rocks on my gas barbecue are increasingly black and greasy looking. What is the best way to clean them?

A: Get rid of the rocks and replace them with man-made ceramic briquettes. You will find briquettes in many respects superior: they sit very close together, so less fats fall through on to the gas burners; their smooth surface means that most of the fats and juices burn off leaving only a small residue, easily dealt with by simply turning them over prior to the next cookout (any fat residue will burn off during the following cooking session and so on).

Otherwise, subject the rock to High for 10 minutes or so

immediately after cooking. This technique, productive but not cost effective, works best if you cover the rock with several layers of heavy-duty aluminium foil and keep the barbecue lid in the closed position. Alternatively, you could boil the rocks in water, to which a small amount of detergent has been added – you will need to allow them to dry thoroughly before re-use.

Q: I have an old 40-gallon oil drum that I should like to convert into a barbecue. A few pointers on how to do this would be useful.

A: First thing is to enlist the help of someone (probably your local garage) in possession of an oxyacetylene burner and ask them to cut the drum into two equal halves lengthwise. You now have the option of converting the halves into two open barbecues, generously giving away one half or using both to make a large barrel barbecue.

To make an open barbecue Construct some form of stable support: easiest would be two pairs of swivel legs, made from steel tube or angle-iron, securely linked, which, when opened, form two Xs, in which to sit the drum half. Drill three or four 1 cm (½ inch) holes, in a group, in the lower half of the drum to help air flow.

To make a barrel barbecue You will have to join the halves together with two, preferably three, strong hinges. To lessen the strain on the hinges, it is a good idea to incorporate stainless-steel wire stays just long enough to allow the lid to open just past the vertical position. Fit some form of handle – preferably with a hardwood grip – to the lid. The leg supports will need to be strong to take the extra weight. Three or four 1 cm (½ inch) holes should be drilled, in a group, in the lid in order to prevent the fire being snuffed out when the lid is in the closed position. You will need to fabricate a charcoal grate from expanded metal (with diamond-shape holes). If you are not able to find any oven-redundant chrome-plated food grills, you could use expanded metal cut to size.

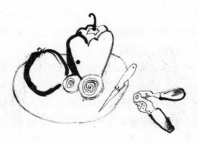

Approximate liquid conversions

British	USA/AUS
4 tablespoons	¼ cup
125 ml (4 fl oz)	½ cup
250 ml (8 fl oz)	1 cup
10 fl oz (½ pint)	1¼ cups
450 ml (¾ pint)	2 cups
600 ml (1 pint)	2½ cups

Approximate solid conversions

British	USA/AUS
500 g (1 lb) butter	2 cups
200 g (7 oz) long grain rice	1 cup
500 g (1 lb) sugar	2 cups
50 g (2 oz) chopped onion	½ cup
50 g (2 oz) soft breadcrumbs	1 cup
125 g (4 oz) dry breadcrumbs	1 cup
500 g (1 lb) plain flour	4 cups
50 g (2 oz) thinly sliced mushrooms	½ cup
125 g (4 oz) grated Cheddar (lightly packed)	1 cup
125 g (4 oz) chopped nuts	1 cup